Congressional Research Service

Asian Carp and the Great Lakes Region

Eugene H. Buck
Specialist in Natural Resources Policy

Harold F. Upton
Analyst in Natural Resources Policy

Charles V. Stern
Specialist in Natural Resources Policy

Cynthia Brougher
Legislative Attorney

July 26, 2012

Congressional Research Service

7-5700

www.crs.gov

R41082

Summary

Four species of non-indigenous Asian carp are expanding their range in U.S. waterways, resulting in a variety of concerns and problems. Three species—bighead, silver, and black carp—are of particular note, based on the perceived degree of environmental concern. Current controversy relates to what measures might be necessary and sufficient to prevent movement of Asian carp from the Mississippi River drainage into the Great Lakes through the Chicago Area Waterway System. Several bills have been introduced in the 112th Congress to direct actions to avoid the possibility of carp becoming established in the Great Lakes.

According to the Great Lakes Fishery Commission, Asian carp pose a significant threat to commercial and recreational fisheries of the Great Lakes. Asian carp populations could expand rapidly and change the composition of Great Lakes ecosystems. Native species could be harmed because Asian carp are likely to compete with them for food and modify their habitat. It has been widely reported that Great Lakes fisheries generate economic activity of approximately $7 billion annually. Although Asian carp introduction is likely to modify Great Lakes ecosystems and cause harm to fisheries, studies forecasting the extent of potential harm are not available. Therefore, it is not possible to provide estimates of potential changes in the regional economy or economic value (social welfare) by lake, species, or fishery.

The locks and waterways of the Chicago Area Waterway System (CAWS) have been a focal point for those debating how to prevent Asian carp encroachment on the Great Lakes. The CAWS is the only navigable link between the Great Lakes and the Mississippi River, and many note the potential of these waterways to facilitate invasive species transfers from one basin to the other. The U.S. Army Corps of Engineers constructed and is currently operating electrical barriers to prevent fish passage through these waterways. In light of recent indications that Asian carp may be present upstream of the barriers, increased federal funding to prevent fish encroachment was announced by the Obama Administration. Part of this funding is being spent by the Corps of Engineers to explore options relating to the "hydrologic separation" of the Great Lakes and Mississippi River drainage basins. The potential closure of navigation structures in the CAWS is of particular interest to both the Chicago area shipping industry and Great Lakes fishery interests.

Since December 2010, Michigan and other Great Lakes states have filed a number of requests for court ordered measures to stop the migration of invasive Asian carp toward Lake Michigan from the Mississippi River basin via the CAWS. The U.S. Supreme Court denied several motions for injunctions to force Illinois, the U.S. Army Corps of Engineers, and the Metropolitan Water Reclamation District of Greater Chicago to take necessary measures to prevent the carp from entering Lake Michigan. Michigan, Minnesota, Ohio, Pennsylvania, and Wisconsin sought a separate order in federal district court seeking similar relief, which was also denied.

In the 112th Congress, language in P.L. 112-74 authorized the Corps of Engineers to take emergency measures to exclude Asian carp from the Great Lakes. In addition, H.R. 892 and S. 471 would direct federal agencies to take measures to control the spread of Asian carp. Notably, each of these bills, as well as H.R. 4406 and S. 2317, would require the Corps of Engineers to complete the Chicago portion of a study on hydrologic separation of the Great Lakes and Mississippi River Basin within 18 months of enactment. H.R. 2432 would require the Corps of Engineers to prepare an economic impact statement before carrying out any federal action relating to the Chicago Area Water System. H.R. 4146 and S. 2164 would authorize the Corps of Engineers to take actions to manage Asian carp traveling up the Mississippi River in Minnesota.

Contents

Figures

Tables

Contacts

Background

Four species of non-indigenous Asian carp are expanding their range in U.S. waterways, resulting in a variety of concerns and problems. Three species—bighead, silver, and black carp—are of particular note, based on the perceived degree of environmental concern. Current controversy relates to what measures might be necessary and sufficient to prevent movement of Asian carp from the Mississippi River drainage into the Great Lakes through the Chicago Area Waterway System. Movement of Asian carp into the Great Lakes is ultimately of concern because increased numbers of carp in the Great Lakes increases the risk that Asian carp will establish reproducing populations in these waters. Several bills have been introduced in the 112th Congress to direct actions to avoid the possibility of carp becoming established in the Great Lakes.

Grass Carp[1]

The grass carp or white amur, *Ctenopharyngodon idella*, was first imported to the United States in 1963 by the U.S. Fish and Wildlife Service for biological control of vegetation in aquatic environments. Grass carp are stocked to biologically control invasive aquatic plants, such as *Hydrilla* and Eurasian water milfoil. Shallow, quiet waters are their typical habitat, and this species easily tolerates waters near freezing. Grass carp initially escaped from the U.S. Fish and Wildlife Service Fish Farming Experimental Station in Stuttgart, AR. By 1970, grass carp had been stocked in lakes and reservoirs throughout the southeast United States and in Arizona, including some that were open to stream systems.[2] It has since spread widely across the country (**Figure 1**), including to four of the Great Lakes. Most grass carp now are stocked as sterile triploids,[3] and grass carp have not established breeding populations in the Great Lakes basin.

Black Carp[4]

The black carp, *Mylopharyngodon piceus*, arrived in the United States in 1973 with silver and bighead carp. Subsequently, this species was imported as a food fish, as the only cost-effective biological control agent to control non-native snails in catfish aquaculture ponds in Arkansas and Mississippi, and as a potential sterile biological control agent for zebra mussels. Of the four species of carp in U.S. waterways, black carp has the most limited known distribution (**Figure 2**).

The preferred habitat of black carp is along the bottom in deep water of large rivers. Owing to this habitat preference for deeper waters, sampling to determine black carp distribution is considered incomplete, since sampling is more difficult in deeper waters. Black carp feed primarily on mussels and snails, and there are concerns that black carp may harm native mollusks, many of which are listed as threatened or endangered under the Endangered Species Act.

---

[1] Information from U.S. Geological Survey Fact Sheet, at http://nas.er.usgs.gov/queries/FactSheet.asp?speciesID=514; and A.J. Mitchell and A.M. Kelly, "The Public Sector Role in the Establishment of Grass Carp in the United States," *Fisheries*, Vol. 31, no. 3 (March 2006):113-121.

[2] F.J. Guscio and E.O. Gangstad, *Research and Planning Conference on the Biological Control of Aquatic Weeds with the White Amur*, prepared for the interagency Research Advisory Committee, Aquatic Plant Control Program, Office of the Chief of Engineers, Department of Army, 1970.

[3] The U.S. Fish and Wildlife Service established a Triploid Grass Carp Inspection Program in 1985 to certify that only genetically triploid (i.e., sterile) grass carp are shipped among 32 states restricting the import of any non-sterile grass carp. For more information on this program, see http://www.fws.gov/policy/aquatichandbook/Volume_9/Volume9.htm.

[4] Information from U.S. Geological Survey Fact Sheet, at http://nas.er.usgs.gov/queries/FactSheet.asp?speciesID=573.

Figure 1. Records of Grass Carp Capture, as of May 24, 2012

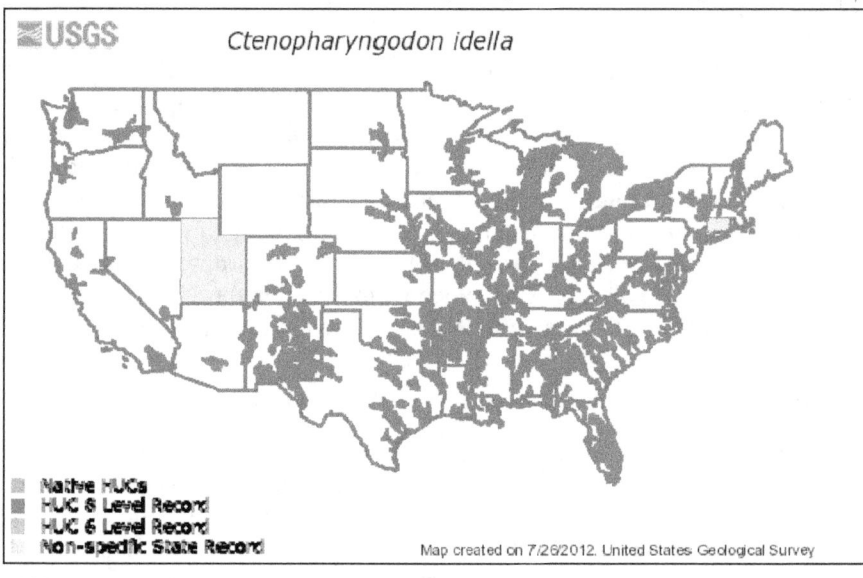

Source: U.S. Geological Survey, Nonindigenous Aquatic Species Fact Sheet on grass carp.

Notes: HUC (Hydrologic Unit Code) indicates to how much of a drainage basin the data apply. HUC 8 = one or more grass carp captured in the drainage subbasin. Records should not be interpreted as indicating the current presence of grass carp in all these areas.

Figure 2. Records of Black Carp Capture, as of May 24, 2012

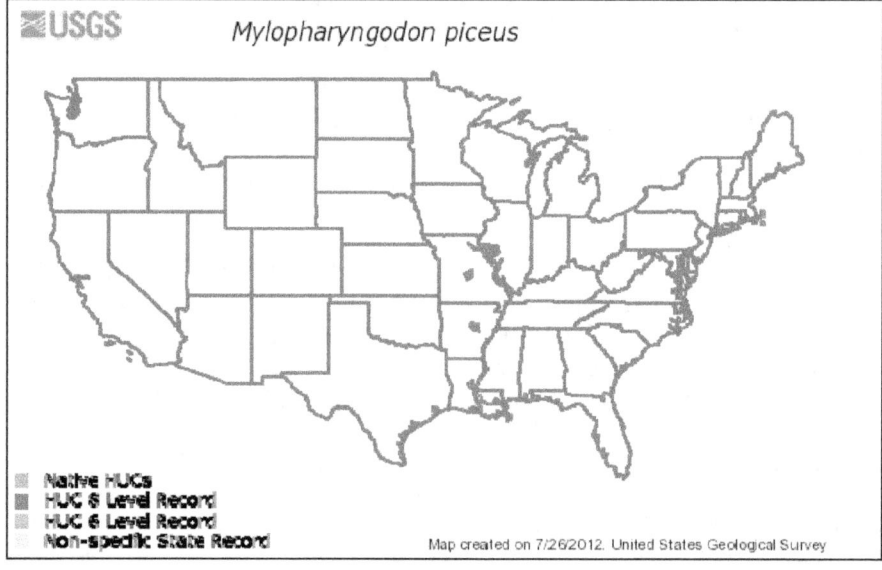

Source: U.S. Geological Survey, Nonindigenous Aquatic Species Fact Sheet on black carp.

Notes: HUC 8 = one or more black carp captured in the drainage subbasin. Records should not be interpreted as indicating the current presence of black carp in all these areas.

Silver Carp[5]

Silver carp, *Hypophthalmichthys molitrix*, were brought into the United States in 1973 under an agreement of maintenance between a private fish farmer and the Arkansas Game and Fish Commission.[6] This species has been used to control phytoplankton (microscopic drifting algae) in nutrient-rich water bodies and is also a food fish. Escapes from a state fish hatchery and from research projects involving use of these fish in municipal sewage systems,[7] as well as possible inclusion of silver carp among other fish shipments, contributed to the spread of this species. Silver carp proved unsuitable for U.S. aquaculture, and were never widely used. The U.S. distribution of silver carp is confined primarily to the Mississippi River drainage, with no record of capture in the Great Lakes (**Figure 3**).

Figure 3. Records of Silver Carp Capture, as of May 24, 2012

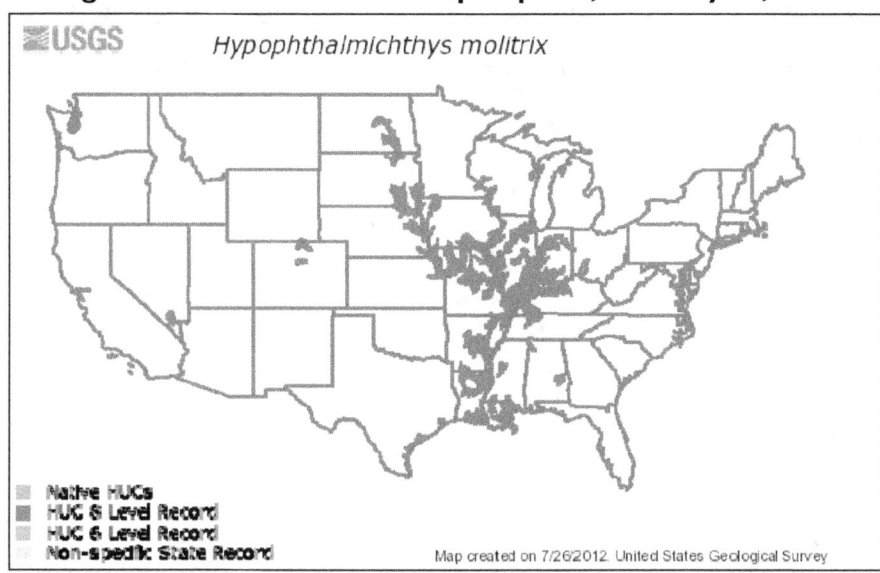

Source: U.S. Geological Survey, Nonindigenous Aquatic Species Fact Sheet on silver carp.

Notes: HUC (Hydrologic Unit Code) indicates to how much of a drainage basin the data apply. HUC 8 = one or more silver carp captured in the drainage subbasin. Records should not be interpreted as indicating the current presence of silver carp in all these areas.

The silver carp is a filter-feeder, capable of consuming large amounts of phytoplankton, zooplankton (small drifting and/or swimming invertebrates), and detritus. Silver carp are easily startled by outboard motors, causing them to jump several feet out of the water.

---

[5] Information from U.S. Geological Survey Fact Sheet, at http://nas.er.usgs.gov/queries/FactSheet.asp?speciesID=549.

[6] W.L. Shelton and R. O. Smitherman, "Exotic Fishes in Warm-Water Aquaculture," *Distribution, Biology, and Management of Exotic Fishes*, W.R. Courtenay, Jr. and J.R. Stauffer, eds., Baltimore, MD: The Johns Hopkins University Press, 1984, p. 262-301.

[7] Scott Henderson, *An Evaluation of Filter Feeding Fishes for Removing Excessive Nutrients and Algae from Wastewater*, U.S. Environmental Protection Agency, Project Summary, EPA-600/S2-83-019, May 1983.

There are no population estimates of silver carp in U.S. waters. However, the population of silver carp in the La Grange Reach of the Illinois River during 2007-2008 was estimated to be about 4,000 fish per river mile, with a biomass of about 19,000 pounds per river mile.[8]

Bighead Carp[9]

Bighead carp, *Hypophthalmichthys nobilis*, were brought into the United States in 1973 under an agreement of maintenance between the Arkansas Game and Fish Commission and a private fish farmer.[10] They proved suitable for U.S. aquaculture[11] and continue to be economically important in Arkansas, Mississippi, and Alabama.[12] This species was discovered in open waters of the Ohio and Mississippi Rivers in the 1980s, probably after escaping from fish hatcheries and/or research projects involving use of these fish in municipal sewage systems.[13] In the United States, bighead carp are found primarily in the Mississippi River drainage. However, a limited number of bighead carp were captured by commercial fishermen in Lake Erie between 1995 and 2003 (**Figure 4**).

Figure 4. Records of Bighead Carp Capture, as of May 24, 2012

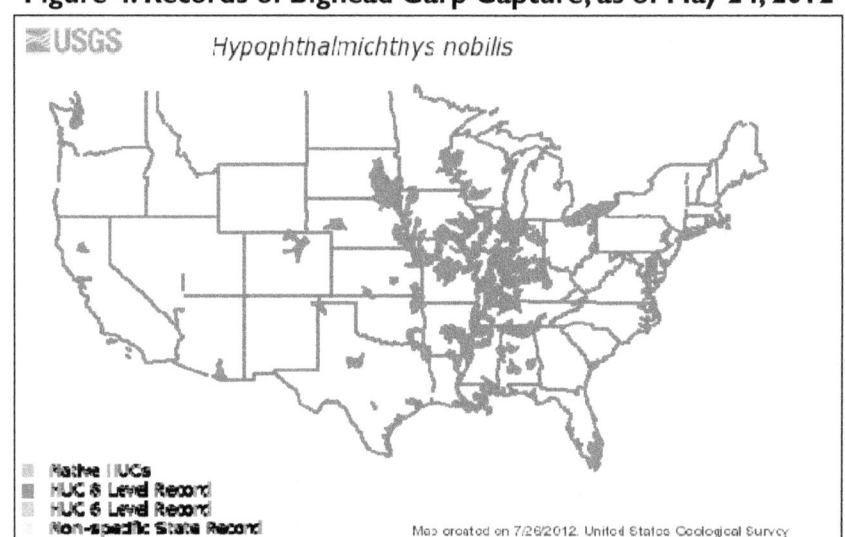

Source: U.S. Geological Survey, Nonindigenous Aquatic Species Fact Sheet on bighead carp.
Notes: HUC (Hydrologic Unit Code) indicates to how much of a drainage basin the data apply. HUC 8 = one or more bighead carp captured in the drainage subbasin. Records should not be interpreted as indicating the current presence of bighead carp in all these areas.

---

[8] Greg G. Sass, et al., "A Mark-Recapture Population Estimate for Invasive Silver Carp (*Hypophthalmichthys molitrix* in the La Grange Reach, Illinois River," *Biological Invasions*, v. 12, no. 3 (2010): 433-436.

[9] Information from U.S. Geological Survey Fact Sheet, at http://nas.er.usgs.gov/queries/FactSheet.asp?speciesID=551.

[10] W.L. Shelton and R. O. Smitherman, "Exotic Fishes in Warm-Water Aquaculture," *Distribution, Biology, and Management of Exotic Fishes*, W.R. Courtenay, Jr. and J.R. Stauffer, eds., Baltimore, MD: The Johns Hopkins University Press, 1984, p. 262-301.

[11] At one time, the market for this species produced by aquaculture was primarily the ethnic live-fish trade in large cities. However, live sale of this species is now prohibited in many cities. For California markets, these fish were killed before entering the state to keep them as fresh as possible. An exception is New York City, where it is still legal to sell live bighead carp, but they must be killed before they leave the store.

[12] This species also was raised previously by aquaculture operations in Kansas and Illinois.

[13] Scott Henderson, *An Evaluation of Filter Feeding Fishes for Removing Excessive Nutrients and Algae from Wastewater*, U.S. Environmental Protection Agency, Project Summary, EPA-600/S2-83-019, May 1983.

Like silver carp, bighead carp typically require large rivers for spawning, but inhabit lakes, backwaters, reservoirs, and other low-current areas during most of their life cycle. They are filter-feeders, consuming primarily phytoplankton and zooplankton.

Managing Non-Native Species

Non-native species that do become established commonly exist at low populations for several generations, after which some begin a period of rapid population growth and range expansion. Although initial captures of wild silver carp were reported in the early 1970s, silver carp only rarely were captured in U.S. rivers until about 1999, after which their population began to grow at an exponential rate. Some suggest that floods in the early 1990s may have provided excellent spawning and recruitment opportunities for silver carp, and stimulated their later exponential growth phase.[14] Field experience in the United States has shown that silver carp generally follow a few years after bighead carp in colonizing new habitat.[15]

Many factors may contribute to the introduction and spread of non-native species. For example, juvenile silver and bighead carp are easily mistaken for native baitfish. Thus, the dumping of unused bait by sport fishermen may contribute to the introduction and spread of these species. In addition, bighead carp (as well as a number of other potentially invasive non-native fish species) have been reared, transported, and traded in large numbers as live fish for human food, especially in large metropolitan areas. Such commerce in bighead carp occurred with relatively limited state and local regulation until recently.

Eradication of non-native species in aquatic environments is difficult and rare, having only occasionally been successful when efforts were focused on small-scale and closed systems like reservoirs, ponds, small locks, and marinas. Since eradication of a non-native species, once it has become established, is unlikely, difficult, and therefore expensive, management more often focuses on preventing troublesome species from entering new habitats, through regulating imports of certain nuisance species, preventing or slowing the spread of already introduced species, and monitoring to detect new invaders when their populations may be localized and at low densities such that eradication might still be possible.[16] While efforts to prevent introduction may be costly, it almost always will be less expensive than continued attempts to eradicate or control non-native species that become established.

---

[14] Duane Chapman, research fisheries biologist, U.S. Geological Survey, Columbia Environmental Research Center, Columbia MO, personal communication, February 26, 2010.

[15] Greg Conover, "The Asian Carp Working Group Update," *ANS Task Force Spring Meeting Minutes*, May 26-27, 2004, p. 35-37; Available at http://www.anstaskforce.gov/Minutes/Spring04_Minutes.pdf.

[16] For more background on prevention and control methods, see CRS Report RL30123, *Invasive Non-Native Species: Background and Issues for Congress*, by M. Lynne Corn et al.

Potential Impacts

Ecological Concerns

Scientists disagree on the ability of Asian carp to thrive in the Great Lakes and the potential damage these fish might cause to Great Lakes ecosystems.[17] According to the Great Lakes Fishery Commission,[18] Asian carp pose a significant threat to fisheries of the Great Lakes.[19] Asian carp populations could expand rapidly and change the composition of Great Lakes ecosystems. Direct ecological effects are likely to result from their various diets: silver carp eat phytoplankton, bighead carp eat zooplankton, black carp eat invertebrates such as snails and mussels, and grass carp eat aquatic plants. Resident Great Lakes fish species could be harmed, because Asian carp are likely to compete with them for food and modify their habitat. Species at greatest risk include native mussels, other aquatic invertebrates, and fishes.[20] As bighead and silver carp have dispersed and migrated within the Mississippi River drainage, these species have out-competed native fish to become the most abundant fish in certain areas.[21] In the Lake Erie basin, the Maumee, Sandusky, and Grand Rivers were determined to be the most likely to be able to support spawning of Asian carp.[22] In July 2012, a Bi-national U.S.-Canadian Asian Carp Risk Assessment concluded that bighead and silver carp pose a substantial environmental risk to the Great Lakes within 20 years, with the risk increasing over time, especially for Lakes Michigan, Huron, and Erie.[23] This assessment further concluded that should bighead and silver carp become established in the Great Lakes, their spread would not likely be limited. Ecological consequences might include competition for planktonic food, leading to reduced growth rates, and recruitment and abundance of fish dependent upon this plankton, as well as reduced abundance of fishes with pelagic, early life stages.

On the other hand, others have predicted that black carp are not likely to become established in the Great Lakes if introduced, while silver carp are predicted neither to spread quickly nor to be perceived as a nuisance in the Great Lakes.[24] Bighead carp were not considered in this analysis.

Furthermore, the Great Lakes today are hardly pristine habitat, with the intentional human introduction of non-native species (e.g., brown and rainbow trout, coho and Chinook salmon) characterizing fishery management of the waters for many years. The intentional and accidental introduction of non-native species has changed this historic ecosystem in many ways, including depletion of previously dominant lake trout and whitefish species. In addition, the ecological changes wrought by non-native species arriving in ship ballast water (e.g., zebra mussels, round goby) and by other means (e.g., lamprey and alewife) have been substantial.

---

[17] See Adam Hinterthuer, "The Explosive Spread of Asian Carp." *BioScience*, v. 62, no. 3 (March 2012): 220-224.

[18] Established in 1954 under the bilateral U.S./Canada Convention on Great Lakes Fisheries.

[19] See http://www.glfc.org/fishmgmt/carp.php.

[20] See http://www.asiancarp.org/rapidresponse/documents/AsianCarp.pdf.

[21] See http://www.glfc.org/fishmgmt/carp.php.

[22] Patrick M. Kocovsky, et al., "Thermal and Hydrologic Suitability of Lake Erie and Its Major Tributaries for Spawning of Asian Carps," *Journal of Great Lakes Research*, v. 38, no. 1 (March 2012): 159-166.

[23] Available at http://www.dfo-mpo.gc.ca/Csas-sccs/publications/resdocs-docrech/2011/2011_114-eng.pdf.

[24] Cynthia S. Kolar and David M. Lodge, "Ecological Predictions and Risk Assessment for Alien Fishes in North America," *Science*, vol. 298 (November 8, 2002), pp. 1233-1236.

Economic Concerns

Recreational and commercial fisheries of the Great Lakes depend on fish populations that could be affected by Asian carp. The primary economic impacts of Asian carp are likely to be related to these fisheries, although concerns have also been raised about potential effects on recreational boating and hunting.[25] Although the net effects are likely to be negative, it is also possible that the introduction of Asian carp to the Great Lakes may provide some utility, such as the development of new commercial and recreational fisheries.[26]

It has been widely reported that Great Lakes fisheries generate U.S. economic activity of approximately $7 billion annually.[27] One should exercise caution in using this figure for assessing public policy alternatives or to make comparisons with the value of other economic sectors. The Great Lakes is composed of many fisheries, each specific to different water bodies, species, and groups of users. Asian carp are likely to affect each lake and areas within lakes to varying degrees because of different biological, chemical, and physical conditions. Anglers will be affected to different degrees depending on local ecological interactions and substitute angling opportunities.

Measures of economic activity such as the $7 billion of economic impacts are only one dimension of economic analysis. The economic input-output studies of the recreational and boating sectors provided below cannot be used to estimate changes in social welfare,[28] to assess trade-offs among public policy alternatives, or to conduct benefit-cost analysis. To more fully understand how society would be affected, valuation studies would be required to estimate the potential changes in social welfare resulting from Asian carp introduction.

Although Asian carp introduction is likely to harm many Great Lakes fisheries, potential changes to ecosystems and the associated economy are not well understood. It is questionable whether accurate predictions of changes by lake, species, and associated fishery are possible. Potential changes resulting from species invasions are difficult to assess because of the underlying complexity of ecological and economic systems. Data and models required to make these assessments are not available and complete assessments would be costly and likely require years of research. The lack of definitive predictions does not mean that the effects of Asian carp introduction would not be significant or that managers should wait to assess the actual effects as Asian carp become established in the Great Lakes. Existing information related to Asian carp movement and population increases in the Mississippi Basin and the magnitude of recreational activities in the Great Lakes indicate that a major threat exists and the effects are likely to be significant.

The economic contributions of recreational and commercial activities on state and regional economies of the Great Lakes region are significant. The economic input-output data cited below measure financial activities associated with the money people spend to buy goods and services on

---

[25] According to the U.S. Fish and Wildlife Service, Asian carp degrade waterfowl habitat and put waterfowl production areas at risk. Reductions of waterfowl populations could decrease hunting opportunities and associated economic impacts from hunting expenditures.

[26] Dan Brannan, "Business Hopes to Sell Invasive Carp to Asians," *The Telegraph* , March 14, 2010.

[27] This discussion only considers the U.S. economy; Canadian fisheries and recreation might also be affected. See the later section "Canadian Concern."

[28] Social welfare is a measure of the well-being of society or of a community. Estimates of changes in social welfare determine whether society loses or gains from a given action.

their fishing trips. Expenditures at businesses that provide goods and services have direct, indirect, and induced effects on business revenues, jobs, and personal income in the local area and at the state level. This approach to assessing recreational fishing is the expenditure and economic impact approach. The following descriptions provide recent economic information, but do not consider the effects of Asian carp introduction.

The Great Lakes' recreational fisheries target perch, black bass, walleye, lake trout, salmon, pike, steelhead, and others. In 2006, approximately 1.5 million anglers fished 17.9 million recreational days on the Great Lakes.[29] These anglers spent an estimated $1.2 billion during Great Lakes fishing trips and $1.3 billion on equipment for activities related to Great Lakes fishing.[30] Economic impacts resulting from these expenditures included more than 58,000 jobs, salaries of $2.1 billion, and total impacts[31] throughout the U.S. economy of slightly more than $7 billion.[32] Great Lakes fisheries also support charter boat fishing businesses that provide recreational fishing services to anglers. In 2002, an estimated 1,746 charter firms made more than 93,000 charter trips in the Great Lakes region.[33] **Table 1** provides a breakdown of angling activity and economic impacts of recreational fishing by state.

In 2008, Great Lakes commercial fishing produced 18.3 million pounds of fish with a landed value[34] of nearly $17 million (**Table 2**).[35] Commercial fisheries are important to many coastal communities, and except for Lake Erie, each lake supports tribal fisheries. Top species are lake whitefish, yellow perch, walleye, chubs, and smelt. For certain species, specific lakes contribute the bulk of commercial landings—including Lake Huron (60% of whitefish), Lake Erie (84% of yellow perch, and 94% of smelt), and Lake Michigan (80% of chubs).[36] Record harvests occurred in 1899, when 120 million pounds were landed in the United States.[37] Landings were dominated by lake herring and chubs (64 million pounds), lake trout (10 million pounds), and yellow perch (10 million pounds).[38] Landings and value of commercial fisheries in the Great Lakes have declined dramatically because of factors such as invasive species, pollution, habitat degradation, overfishing, competition with imports, personal tastes and preferences, and regulatory changes.

---

[29] U.S. Department of the Interior, Fish and Wildlife Service, and U.S. Department of Commerce, Census Bureau, *2006 National Survey of Fishing, Hunting, and Wildlife-Associated Recreation*, Washington, DC, 2007.

[30] Southwick Associates, *Sportfishing in America: An Economic Engine and Conservation Powerhouse*, American Sportfishing Association, Multistate Conservation Grant Program, 2007. Hereinafter cited as "Southwick Associates 2007."

[31] Total impacts include direct, indirect, and induced impacts as money is cycled through the economy, in this case as a result of expenditures on recreational fishing equipment and trips.

[32] Southwick Associates 2007.

[33] See http://www.glerl.noaa.gov/seagrant/FEE/05-504-Economics.pdf.

[34] In this case, landed value is the amount paid to fishermen at the dock.

[35] U.S. Department of Commerce, National Marine Fisheries Service, *Fisheries of the United States 2008*, Silver Spring, MD, July 2009.

[36] Ronald E. Kinnunen, *Great Lakes Commercial Fisheries*, Michigan Sea Grant Extension, Marquette, MI, August 2003.

[37] Norman S. Baldwin, Robert W. Saafeld, and Margaret A. Ross, et al., *Commercial Fish Production in the Great Lakes 1867-1977*, Great Lakes Fishery Commission, Technical Report No. 3, Ann Arbor, MI, September 1979. Hereinafter cited as Great Lakes Fishery Commission 1979.

[38] Great Lakes Fishery Commission 1979.

Table 1. Great Lakes Recreational Fishing Activity and Economic Impacts in 2006

States	Anglers	Days Fished	Retail Sales (000s)	Salaries (000s)	Jobs	Total Impact (000s)
Illinois	56,000	728,000	$93,589	$55,158	1,511	$175,074
Indiana	46,000	759,000	$224,588	$117,321	4,170	$394,866
Michigan	461,000	6,981,000	$562,654	$312,197	8,283	$1,001,641
Minnesota	48,000	272,000	NR	NR	NR	NR
New York	247,000	2,060,000	$213,174	$122,147	3,288	$369,194
Ohio	328,000	2,807,000	$480,482	$248,301	9,915	$801,817
Pennsylvania	85,000	598,000	$399,342	$213,921	5,200	$725,705
Wisconsin	235,000	3,705,000	$315,336	$159,420	6,153	$528,274
Totals (Great Lakes States)	**1,506,000**	**17,910,000**	**$2,289,165**	**$1,228,465**	**38,520**	**$3,996,571**
Totals (United States)			**$2,524,266**	**$2,189,490**	**58,291**	**$7,089,230**

Sources: U.S. Department of the Interior, Fish and Wildlife Service, and U.S. Department of Commerce, Census Bureau, *2006 National Survey of Fishing, Hunting, and Wildlife-Associated Recreation*, Washington, DC, 2007. Southwick Associates, *Sportfishing in America: An Economic Engine and Conservation Powerhouse*, American Sportfishing Association, Multistate Conservation Grant Program, 2007.

Notes: Great Lakes fishing includes lakes Superior, Michigan, Huron, Ontario, Erie, and St. Clair, connecting waters, and fishing in tributaries for smelt, steelhead, and salmon. Minnesota economic impacts were not reported (NR) because of small sample size. Illinois (<10), Indiana, and Pennsylvania estimates should also be used with caution because of small sample sizes (10 to 30). Retail sales include trip and equipment expenditures. Equipment expenditures were prorated according to how and where equipment such as boats were used. United States totals include economic impacts outside Great Lakes states that resulted from trip and equipment expenditures for Great Lakes fishing.

Table 2. Great Lakes Commercial Fishing Landings and Revenue in 2008

State	Landings (pounds)	Revenue
Michigan	9,998,000	$7,448,000
Minnesota	318,000	$158,000
New York	44,000	$65,000
Ohio	4,493,000	$5,315,000
Pennsylvania	50,000	$140,000
Wisconsin	3,376,000	$3,641,000
Total	**18,279,000**	**$16,767,000**

Source: U.S. Department of Commerce, National Marine Fisheries Service, *Fisheries of the United States 2008*, Silver Spring, MD, July 2009. p.6.

There are 4.3 million boats registered in the Great Lakes states, and it has been estimated that 911,000 operate on the Great Lakes.[39] When disturbed by a boat motor, silver carp may jump as high as 10 feet out of the water. In parts of the Mississippi River drainage, silver carp have caused injuries and damaged equipment when large fish have jumped into moving boats. Silver carp also

---

[39] Great Lakes Commission, *Great Lakes Recreational Boating's Economic Punch*, Ann Arbor, MI, 2004. Hereinafter cited as "Great Lakes Commission 2004."

could injure boaters and water-skiers and detract from boating in the Great Lakes. As in the case of fisheries, predictions of the potential magnitude of economic effects on Great Lakes boating are not available.

In 2004, the U.S. Army Corps of Engineers in partnership with the Great Lakes Commission undertook a study of recreational boating in the Great Lakes states. Recreational boaters spent approximately $9.8 billion during trips and $5.7 billion on craft in Great Lakes states.[40] Economic results from these expenditures included more than 246,000 jobs and salaries of $6.5 billion. **Table 3** provides economic measures of boating on Great Lakes states. The study found that a significant share of boating expenditures took place at Great Lakes marinas. It is also likely that a significant portion of boating expenditures are related to fishing activity.

Table 3. Annual Economic Impact of Boating on Great Lakes States in 2003

(includes all registered boats and boating in Great Lakes states)

State	Boats (000s)	Sales (000s)	Jobs	Salaries (000s)
Illinois	360,252	$1,958,000	22,407	$678,000
Indiana	216,145	$2,203,000	30,437	$710,000
Michigan	953,554	$3,905,000	51,329	$1,342,000
Minnesota	845,094	$3,709,000	49,060	$1,247,000
New York	528,094	$2,749,000	28,901	$987,000
Ohio	413,048	$1,959,000	26,148	$656,000
Pennsylvania	355,235	$71,000	1,195	$24,000
Wisconsin	610,800	$2,493,000	36,640	$825,000
Total	**4,282,222**	**$19,047,000**	**246,117**	**$6,479,000**

Source: Great Lakes Commission, *Great Lakes Recreational Boating's Economic Punch*, Ann Arbor, MI, 2004.

Social Concerns

The introduction of Asian carp to the Great Lakes, potentially changing lake ecosystems from "salmon and trout dominated" to "carp dominated," has the potential to damage the public image of these lakes and to lower the feeling of "well being" and pride of area residents.[41] As such, the introduction of these species could reduce the social value of lake-related activities.

The popularity of live Asian carp in some ethnic markets continues to stimulate illegal transport of these fish across state and international borders. In February 2012, Canadian border enforcement personnel intercepted the third illegal shipment of live Asian carp in two months and the fifth in a year. These fish allegedly originated from fish farms in the southern United States and were bound for Toronto.[42]

---

[40] Great Lakes Commission 2004.

[41] For example, see John Schneider, "Asian Carp's Threat Goes Far Beyond Economics," *Lansing State Journal*, June 3, 2010; available at http://www.lansingstatejournal.com/article/20100603/COLUMNISTS09/6030341.

[42] See http://www.eenews.net/Greenwire/print/2012/03/27/11.

The Chicago Area Waterway System (CAWS)

The Chicago Area Waterway System (CAWS) is a segment of the Illinois Waterway in northeastern Illinois and northwestern Indiana. The Illinois Waterway is a 327-mile channel running from Chicago to St. Louis. It is maintained at a minimum depth of 9 feet by the U.S. Army Corps of Engineers (hereinafter referred to as the Corps).[43] It is the only navigable link between two of the largest freshwater drainage basins in the world, the Great Lakes and the Mississippi River. The CAWS portion of the Illinois Waterway includes modified rivers, locks, canals and other structures that control the flow of water through the Chicago metropolitan area. It has recently received attention for its potential to provide a pathway for Asian carp to migrate from the Mississippi River and its tributaries into the Great Lakes. The system of projects comprising the CAWS is shown in **Figure 5**.

Figure 5. Chicago Area Waterway System and Lake Michigan

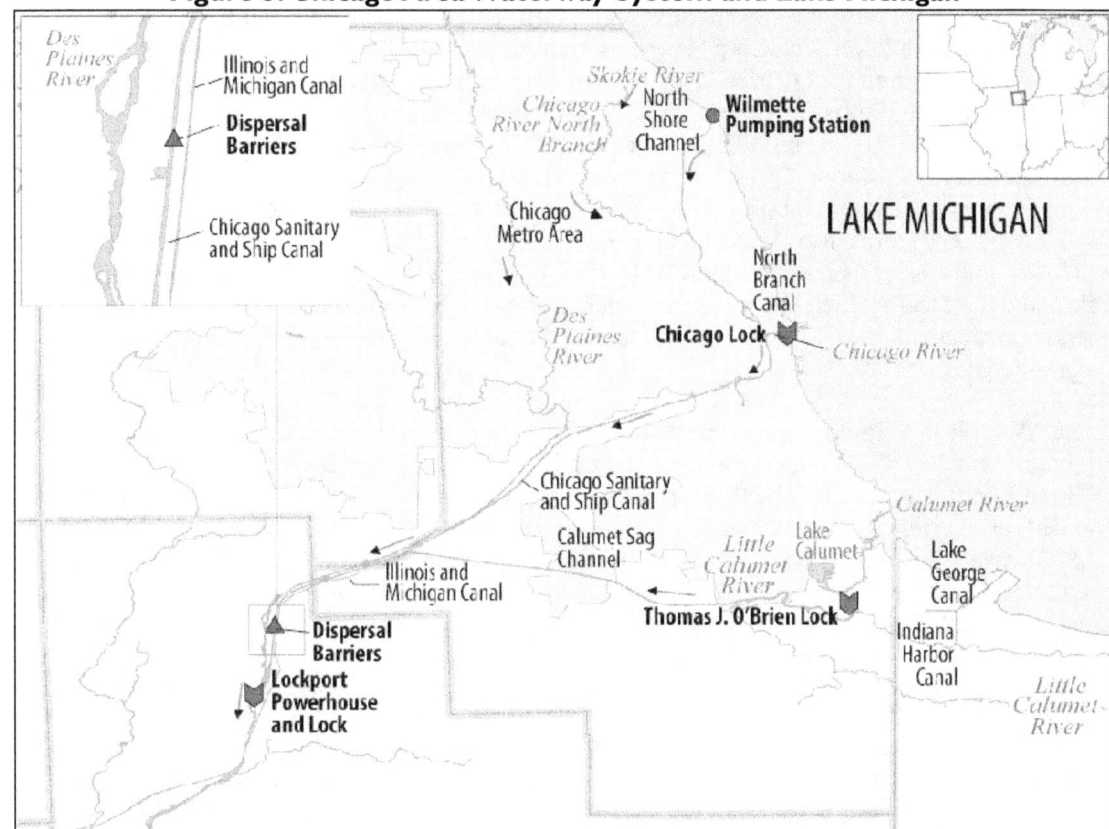

Source: Adapted by the Congressional Research Service, February 2010.

---

[43] Although the Corps has the primary authority to maintain the CAWS for navigation, multiple federal, state, and local entities also possess authorities that must be considered in the context of management actions in the CAWS. Some of these entities include the state of Illinois, the Metropolitan Water and Reclamation District of Greater Chicago, the City of Chicago, the Fish and Wildlife Service, the Environmental Protection Agency, and the U.S. Coast Guard.

Historically, an important geologic feature in the Chicago area's watershed was the Chicago Portage. The Chicago Portage separated the drainage basins of the Mississippi River and the Great Lakes prior to modification of these waterways. These bodies of water were first artificially connected for navigation in 1848 through a privately constructed 97-mile canal connecting the Chicago River to the Illinois River. This canal, known as the Illinois and Michigan (I&M) Canal, was maintained for commercial use from 1848 to 1933. It was eventually replaced by the network of canals and locks that comprises the CAWS.[44] Canals within the CAWS today include the Chicago Sanitary and Ship Canal (or CSSC, completed in 1900), the North Shore Channel (completed in 1910) and the Cal-Sag Channel (completed in 1922). During construction of these canals, the flows of the Chicago River and the Calumet River were also permanently reversed away from Lake Michigan and toward the Mississippi River drainage basin through structural modifications and pumping.[45] The altered flow of the rivers prevented sewage discharge into the canals from contaminating Chicago's drinking water supply intakes on Lake Michigan.

In recent years, the locks of the CAWS have become a focal point for those debating how to prevent invasive species (and specifically, Asian carp) encroachment between the Great Lakes and the Mississippi River. The Corps operates multiple lock sites that connect the CAWS to the Great Lakes, including the O'Brien Lock (on the Cal-Sag Channel) and the Chicago Lock (on the Chicago River; see **Figure 5**). Both of these locks include sluice gates operated by the Metropolitan Water Reclamation District of Greater Chicago (MWRD) that can provide flood control in severe rainstorms.[46] The MWRD independently owns and operates a third site (the Wilmette pumping station) on the North Shore Channel that directly connects the CAWS to the Great Lakes. The Corps also owns and operates the lock at Lockport Powerhouse and Lock, which is southwest of Chicago on the CSSC. (See **Figure 5**.) Due to its distance from the Great Lakes and the fact that the Corp's electric fish barriers (see below section "Electric Barriers") operate upstream on the CSSC, this third lock has not been as prominent in recent invasive species debates.

The CAWS plays a significant role in the region's commercial and recreational navigation, although estimates of the full economic value of the locks within the CAWS (in particular, O'Brien Lock) vary widely. The Chicago Lock, one of the country's busiest locks for traffic, handled 36,256 vessels and conducted 11,599 lockages in 2008.[47] The O'Brien Lock handled 17,532 vessels and conducted 6,310 lockages in 2008.[48] While most of the traffic on the Chicago Lock is recreational, the transit of commodity-laden commercial barges is higher at O'Brien Lock, which allows for shippers to offload onto deepwater vessels.[49] Statistics from the Corps

---

[44] Today the I&M Canal remains open as a state park site. The I&M Canal's potential to move Asian carp into other CAWS canals has been an additional item of discussion in recent invasive species debates.

[45] The canal was designed to run southwest from Lake Michigan toward the Mississippi at a small gradient.

[46] The Corps and the MWRD coordinate during severe rainstorms, and may open both the locks themselves and the sluice gates to allow for discharge of floodwaters into Lake Michigan to prevent flooding of downtown Chicago. This last occurred in 2008.

[47] For additional information, see http://www.ndc.iwr.usace.army.mil/lpms/pdf/lpmsstat_v3.pdf.

[48] U.S. Army Corps of Engineers, *Waterborne Commerce Statistics Center*, 2008. http://www.ndc.iwr.usace.army.mil/lpms/lock2008web.htm.

[49] Ibid. According to Corps statistics, approximately 6.8 million tons in bulk commodities transported through the O'Brien Lock in 2008, while 105,000 tons of commodities were transported through the Chicago Lock in 2008. For additional analysis of vessel movement and lockages based on Corps data, see Joel Brammeier, Irwin Polls, and Scudder Mackey, *Preliminary Feasibility of Ecological Separation of the Mississippi River and the Great Lakes to Prevent the Transfer of Aquatic Invasive Species*, Alliance for the Great Lakes, 2008 Project Completion Report, Chicago, IL, November 2008, pp. 50-55.

---

indicate that approximately 7 million tons worth of commodities move through O'Brien lock annually, including bulk quantities of sand and gravel, coal, and steel.[50]

Additional analysis, including a comparison of alternative means of freight transit, is necessary to fully understand the value of the locks to the region. In response to an estimate by the Corps that shippers saved approximately $192 million by using the O'Brien and Chicago locks in 2008 (or an addition of approximately $27 per ton of freight shipped), the state of Michigan commissioned a study which concluded that the locks are of a considerably less value (thus any closure of locks would have a minimal impact). The Michigan study estimated that a shift from barge to overland shipping would result in additional costs of approximately $64 million-$69 million annually, or approximately $10 per ton.[51] This study was criticized by the Illinois Chamber of Commerce, which published several academic critiques of the Michigan study, as well as a separate study estimating a much higher cost associated with lock closure.[52] In contrast to the Michigan Study, the Illinois Chamber of Commerce study estimated a total cost of $530 million-$580 million annually over the next eight years for lock closure, and a net cost to the Chicago economy of $4.7 billion over a 20-year horizon.[53] The two studies differ considerably in their treatment of several important assumptions, including those related to both direct and indirect costs for the transition to overland shipping in the areas around the locks. The studies have ramifications for ongoing actions to prevent Asian carp, including any decision by the federal government to permanently separate the drainage basins.[54]

Federal Response to Asian Carp

Response to the spread of Asian carp can generally be divided into two categories: actions occurring before and after 2010. Prior to 2010, Congress directed the Corps and other agencies to undertake several specific actions to block the downstream passage of Asian carp in the CAWS. This work was largely conducted by the Corps with planning coordination and funding from other agencies. Additionally, the federal government has been engaged in long-term, nationwide planning and management of Asian carp under authorities codified in the Nonindigenous Aquatic Nuisance Prevention and Control Act of 1990 (P.L. 101-646, as amended) and other statutes.[55] These actions were conducted by the Aquatic Nuisance Species Task Force (ANS Task Force), chaired by the Fish and Wildlife Service (FWS) and the National Oceanic and Atmospheric Administration (NOAA), with support provided by various other agencies, including the U.S. Environmental Protection Agency (EPA), the U.S. Geological Survey (USGS), and the Corps.

---

[50] See U.S. Army Corps of Engineers, *Waterborne Commerce of the United States, Calendar Year 2008, Part 3— Waterways and Harbors, Great Lakes,* IWR-WCUS-08-03, Alexandria, VA, 2008. Available at http://www.iwr.usace.army.mil/ndc/wcsc/pdf/wcusgl08.pdf.

[51] The study was included as an appendix to Michigan's recent Supreme Court filing, and is available at http://www.michigan.gov/documents/ag/1-Appendix-Renewed_Motion_310133_7.pdf. For more information on this litigation, see the "Litigation" section of this report.

[52] Documents available at http://www.ilchamber.org/lockclosingstudy.html.

[53] Joseph P. Schwieterman, An Analysis of the Economic Effects of Terminating Operations at the Chicago River Controlling Works and the O'Brien Locks On the Chicago Area Waterway System, DePaul University, Chicago, IL, April 7, 2010, at http://www.ilchamber.org/documents/lockstudy/ DePaul%20University%20Study%20on%20Terminating%20Lock%20Operations.pdf.

[54] The status of the federal efforts to study this issue is discussed in the below section "Asian Carp Control Strategy Framework."

[55] 16 U.S.C. § 4701.

Due to the increasing profile of Asian carp and its potential establishment in the Great Lakes, efforts to impede the spread of Asian carp have recently intensified. The White House has prioritized the issue, and the Commission on Environmental Quality (CEQ) announced an inter-agency Asian Carp Control Framework in early 2010. The framework outlined actions and funding to build on existing activities, as well as significant new funding for a wide array of state and federal activities intended to combat the spread of Asian carp. Total funding for Asian carp activities since the announcement of the framework has exceeded $100 million, with the majority of this funding derived from the EPA Great Lakes Restoration Initiative. Furthermore, in September 2010 the White House named a director (or "tsar") to oversee these federal efforts.

Pre-2010 Response Efforts

Prevention in the CAWS

Electric Barriers

In the National Invasive Species Act of 1996 (P.L. 104-332), Congress directed the Corps and the ANS Task Force to investigate environmentally sound methods to prevent the dispersal of aquatic nuisance species from the Great Lakes into the Mississippi River drainage.[56] In response, an advisory panel of federal, state, local, and international representatives (known as the Dispersal Barrier Panel) recommended an electronic dispersal barrier demonstration project at the southwestern end of the CSSC north of Lockport Powerhouse and Lock (see **Figure 5**) as the preferred short-term method to stop the movement of invasive species through the CAWS.[57] This type of barrier uses steel cables secured to the bottom of the canal to create a pulsating field of electricity that discourages fish from passing. It was selected based on projected cost, likelihood of success, environmental impacts, commercial availability, permit requirements, and effect on existing canal uses. The barrier was completed in 2001 and became operational in 2002.[58] This barrier experiences occasional power outages,[59] raising concerns that Asian carp might use these opportunities to migrate through the area.

Around the same time the dispersal barrier became operational, rapid upstream encroachment of Asian carp toward Lake Michigan was becoming a management concern for the Fish and Wildlife Service. As a result, the demonstration barrier became the default method to prevent short-term encroachment for Asian carp. Based on subsequent experience and testing, the Dispersal Barrier Panel determined that the demonstration barrier should be upgraded into a stronger, more permanent barrier (Barrier I), and that construction of a second large barrier (Barrier II) would

---

[56] The waters of the CAWS were widely noted to be polluted and oxygen-deprived through the early 1980s. These conditions likely prevented the spread of aquatic species through the area over the earlier history of the CAWS. Recent efforts to clean up the waterway have also made possible the survival of many species in the area, including invasive species.

[57] 16 U.S.C. § 4722(i)(3). Although the barrier was authorized and designed to repel multiple aquatic invasive species, the primary goal of the original barrier was to impede the downstream movement of round goby from the Great Lakes to the Mississippi River basin. Because of funding and construction delays, the demonstration barrier was not operational in time to prevent this movement, and round goby were found downstream of the barrier site in 1999.

[58] A full history of the demonstration barrier, including the rationale for the preferred barrier technology, is available at http://www.seagrant.wisc.edu/ais/default.aspx?tabid=1543.

[59] For example, see http://www.brown.senate.gov/newsroom/press/release/after-electronic-asian-carp-barriers-fail-brown-renews-call-for-permanent-hydrological-separation_to-prevent-invasive-species-from-reaching-lake-erie.

---

provide additional protection through redundancy in the barrier system. These recommendations were subsequently authorized by Congress.[60]

Preliminary repairs to Barrier I were completed in October 2008, and the Corps plans to make Barrier I permanent and enhance its operating parameters after Barrier II is complete. Barrier II is located approximately 800 feet downstream from Barrier I, and has two sets of electrical arrays (known as Barriers IIA and IIB). Construction of Barrier IIA began in 2004, and this part of the barrier became permanently operational in 2009 at a total cost of approximately $10 million. Barrier IIB was completed in 2010, at a cost of approximately $13 million.[61] In recent budget requests, the Corps has estimated the cost to operate these barriers at approximately $7.25 million.[62]

Federal agencies have also coordinated rapid response activities to supplement the barrier protection system through the Asian Carp Regional Coordinating Committee (ACRCC), formed in 2009.[63] The ACRCC, led by Council on Environmental Quality, includes representatives from federal agencies, as well as some state and local government organizations. To date, the most visible action by the committee have been chemical treatments on the CSSC (December 1-7, 2009) and the Little Calumet River (May 20-27, 2010). For the CSSC action, more than 450 individuals were involved in the mass rotenone treatment of a 5.7-mile stretch of the CSSC while Barrier IIA was taken down for scheduled maintenance. This effort located a single bighead carp, 500 feet above the Lockport Powerhouse and Lock and downstream from the electric barriers.[64]

Other Prevention

In recent appropriations acts, Congress has generally provided Corps with one-year authority to implement other emergency actions under §3061 of the Water Resources Development Act of 2007 (WRDA 2007, P.L. 110-114).[65] In addition to building the electrical barriers, in WRDA 2007 Congress directed the Corps to study other means to prevent the spread of Asian carp through the CAWS, including the range of options for technologies to prevent passage beyond the electrical barriers.[66] In response to this directive, the Corps initiated a number of studies. First, in

---

[60] The demonstration barrier was originally authorized in the National Invasive Species Act of 1996 (P.L. 104-332) and its funding level was increased in Emergency Supplemental Appropriations Act for Defense, the Global War on Terror, and Hurricane Recovery, 2006 (P.L. 109-234). Funding for Barrier II was first provided as an environmental restoration project under WRDA 1986 (P.L. 99-662, §1135) in 2002 and required a local cost sharing partner. The project was subsequently authorized at a level of $9 million in the District of Columbia Appropriations Act, 2005 (P.L. 108-335, § 345). In WRDA 2007 (P.L. 110-114, §3061), Congress consolidated the multiple authorizations for barrier construction and authorized the Corps to permanently operate both barriers at a 100% federal cost.

[61] Personal Communication with Charles Shea, Dispersal Barrier Project Director, Army Corps of Engineers, Chicago District, February 24, 2010.

[62] Office of the Assistant Secretary of the Army, *FY 2011 Civil Works Budget for the U.S. Army Corps of Engineers.*, Washington, DC, February 2010, p. LRD-132.

[63] See http://www.asiancarp.us/.

[64] Illinois Department of Natural Resources, *Bighead Asian Carp Found in Chicago Sanitary and Ship Canal*, December 3, 2009. Available at http://dnr.state.il.us/pubaffairs/2009/December/asianCarp3Dec2009.htm. At the time, this finding was significant for its confirmation of Asian carp presence in the CSSC. In June, a fish was discovered upstream of the barriers in Lake Calumet. For more information, see "Monitoring" section.

[65] Most recently, Congress extended the Corps emergency authorities in §126 of the enacted appropriations bill for FY2010 (P.L. 111-85).

[66] See 121 Stat. 1121. The Corps is studying four areas in this regard: optimal operating parameters for the barriers, ANS barrier bypass, ANS human transfer, and ANS abundance reduction.

January 2010, the Corps produced a study (known as the Interim I study) that recommended a network of concrete and chain link barricades to deter fish passage over the Des Plaines River during flooding or through culverts connecting the CSSC to the I&M canal.[67] This project was built with approximately $13 million in funding and was completed in 2010. The Corps also conducted a separate study (Interim II study) on optimal operating parameters for the electrical barriers.

The Corps conducted a third study (Interim III study) exploring how its existing locks and other structures could be operated to minimize the likelihood of Asian carp infestation, and has convened meetings with navigation interests on potential operational changes for these structures. The Interim III study, released in June 2010, concluded that partial changes in operating parameters would not be beneficial in slowing Asian carp migration; however, the Corps plans to install fish screens on certain sluice gates and modify operations to provide lock closure during chemical and other control efforts.[68] An additional study (Interim IIIa study) focused on other deterrent measures that could be quickly employed to prevent Asian carp migration into the Great Lakes.[69] This study, completed in April 2010, concluded that a deterrent combining acoustic air bubble barrier technology and strobe lights (ABS deterrent) would be the best available measure to reduce Asian carp migration risk, and noted eight candidate sites at which the ABS deterrent could be utilized.

Monitoring

Prior to 2010, the Corps and other agencies, including the FWS, EPA, and USGS contributed resources toward monitoring efforts to evaluate the presence and movements of Asian carp in the CAWS. In addition to conventional sampling methods such as electrofishing and netting, the Corps worked with the University of Notre Dame to conduct an experimental fish sampling method known as environmental DNA (eDNA) testing. This method filters water samples, then extracts fragments of shed DNA to search for genetic markers unique to Asian carp.[70] While few Asian carp have been located upstream of the barriers using conventional sampling methods, an increasing number of positive eDNA test results for silver carp from multiple locations upstream

---

[67] U.S. Army Corps of Engineers—Chicago District, *Interim I Dispersal Barrier Bypass Risk Reduction Study & Integrated Environmental Assessment*, Final Report, Chicago, IL, January 2010. Available at http://www.lrc.usace.army.mil/pao/ANS_DispersalBarrierEfficacyStudy_Interim_I_FINAL.pdf.

[68] U.S. Army Corps of Engineers—Chicago District, Interim III Dispersal Barrier Efficacy Study: Modified Structures and Operations, Illinois and Chicago Area Waterways, Risk Reduction Study and Integrated Environmental Assessment, Final Report, Chicago, IL, June 2, 2010. p iii. Available at http://www.lrc.usace.army.mil/pao/02June2010_InterimIII.pdf. Notably, the Corps did not consider extended lock closure (i.e., more than two months) under this study.

[69] U.S. Army Corps of Engineers—Chicago District, Interim IIIA Dispersal Barrier Efficacy Study: Modified Fish Dispersal Deterrents, Illinois and Chicago Waterways Risk Reduction Study and Integrated Environmental Assessment, Chicago, IL, April 2010. Available at http://www.lrc.usace.army.mil/pao/02June2010_InterimIIIA.pdf.

[70] An audit of eDNA methodology by EPA in February 2010 concluded that the technique is sufficiently reliable and robust in reporting a pattern of detection that should be considered actionable in a management context. See U.S. Congress, House Committee on Transportation and Infrastructure, Subcommittee on Water Resources and Environment, *Statement of Professor David Lodge, Director, Center for Aquatic Conservation,* hearing on Asian Carp and the Great Lakes, 111th Cong., 2nd sess., February 8, 2010. Appendix: Laboratory Audit Report, Lodge Laboratory, Department of Biological Sciences, University of Notre Dame. See also Christopher L. Jerde, et al., "Sight-Unseen Detection of Rare Aquatic Species Using Environmental DNA," *Conservation Letters,* v. 4, no. 2 (April/May 2011): 150-157.

---

suggest that they may be present on the lake side of the barriers. In addition, recent reports indicate positive DNA test results for both silver and bighead carp from Lake Erie.[71]

Nationwide Asian Carp Management

Separate from efforts focusing on short-term prevention and other actions in the CAWS, the ANS task force has studied and initiated a number of nationwide management actions through its Asian Carp Working Group. Beginning around 2001, the working group requested and co-funded USGS risk assessments of multiple Asian carp species that found a high potential for black, silver, and bighead carp to become established in the United States.[72] In response to these findings, FWS listed black and silver carp as injurious under the Lacey Act in 2007.[73] On December 7, 2010, the President signed P.L. 111-307, which listed bighead carp as injurious under the Lacey Act.

Also in 2007, FWS authored a study, *Management and Control Plan for Bighead, Black, Grass, and Silver Carps in the United States*, produced in collaboration with federal and non-federal stakeholders. The final plan outlines seven broad goals (divided into 133 short- and long-term recommendations) that would contribute to a goal of extermination of wild Asian carp. Recommendations in that report include a wide array of methods, including those intended to stop Asian carp encroachment (such as electric barriers, bubble curtains, and sonic barriers to control carp movement) as well as those that would eliminate wild Asian carp populations outright (including concentrated fishing operations, genetic manipulation, and pheromone baiting).[74]

Recent Developments

Asian Carp Control Strategy Framework

Several recent developments have raised the profile of the Asian carp issue. As previously mentioned, eDNA testing in 2009 and 2010 indicated that it is likely that Asian carp are present at multiple locations upstream of the electric barriers. Additionally, on June 23, 2010, the Asian Carp Regional Coordinating Committee announced the catch of a live bighead carp at Lake Calumet (upstream of the electric barriers, between O'Brien Lock and Lake Michigan) by a

---

[71] See http://abcnews.go.com/US/wireStory/asian-carp-dna-found-year-lake-erie-samples-16775132.

[72] See Leo G. Nico and J. D. Williams, *Black Carp: A Biological Synopsis and Updated Risk Assessment*, U.S. Geological Survey, Final Report to the Risk Assessment and Management Committee of the ANSTF., Gainesville, FL, 2001, available at http://www.fisheries.org/html/publications/catbooks/x51032C.shtml; and C. S. Kolar, D. C. Chapman, and W. R. Courtenay et al., *Asian Carps of the Genus Hypophthalmichthys (Pisces, Cyprinidae):A Biological Synopsis and Environmental Risk Assessment*, U.S. Geological Survey, Report to the Fish and Wildlife Service, LaCrosse, WI, 2005, available at http://www.fws.gov/contaminants/OtherDocuments/ ACBSRAFinalReport2005.pdf.

[73] The Lacey Act, 16 U.S.C. §§ 3371-3378, makes it unlawful to import, export, sell, acquire, or purchase fish, wildlife or plants taken, possessed, transported, or sold (1) in violation of U.S. or Indian law or (2) in interstate or foreign commerce involving any fish, wildlife, or plants taken, possessed or sold in violation of state or foreign law. Under this law, designated injurious species are identified at 50 C.F.R. § 16. See also http://www.anstaskforce.gov/Documents/ Injurious_Wildlife_Fact_Sheet_2007.pdf.

[74] Greg Conover, Rob Simmonds, and Michelle Whalen, *Management and Control Plan for Bighead, Black, Grass, and Silver Carps in the United States,* Aquatic Nuisance Species Task Force, Asian Carp Working Group, Washington, DC, November 2007.

---

fisherman under contract with the Illinois Department of Natural Resources.[75] The finding was significant, as it represented the first live Asian carp located upstream of the barriers.

In response to the increased attention on the issue, on February 8, 2010, the White House convened a Summit for Great Lakes governors on the threat of Asian carp. This meeting focused on defining strategies to combat the spread of Asian carp and improving coordination and effective response across all levels of government. At this summit, the Obama Administration unveiled a framework, known as the Asian Carp Control Strategy Framework (referred to here as the framework).[76] The framework was subsequently finalized and has been updated multiple times.

The original framework built on the existing work by federal agencies (including barrier operations and monitoring) and outlined future actions and new funding sources to eliminate the threat of Asian carp in the Great Lakes. The 2010 framework identified 32 federally funded actions and $78.5 million in funding, of which $58 million is from the President's GLRI (funded by EPA).[77] In 2011, the framework was updated to add 13 new actions, including additional eDNA testing, as well as other new biological controls and monitoring. The updated framework for 2011 maintains a heavy reliance on the GLRI for funding.[78] In FY2012, the updated strategy framework anticipated about $51.7 million in federal funding.[79]

The 45 actions in the most recent framework may be separated into the following general categories:[80]

- Targeted Monitoring and Assessment Above and Below the Electric Barrier System,

- Commercial Harvesting and Removal Action Below the Barrier System,

- Barrier Action and Waterway Separation Measures,

- Great Lakes Mississippi River Inter-Basin Study,

- Research and Technology Development,

- eDNA Analysis and Refinement,

- Funding Opportunities and Agency Preparation Activities, and

- Other Support Activities.

---

[75] See http://asiancarp.org/Wordpress/news/bighead-asian-carp-found-in-chicago-area-waterway-system/.

[76] See .

[77] For a complete summary of the 2010 recommendations, see Asian Carp Regional Coordinating Committee, *Asian Carp Control Strategy Framework,* May 2010, http://www.asiancarp.org/Documents/AsianCarpControlStrategyFrameworkMay2010.pdf.

[78] The 2011 Framework identifies $46 million in funding, of which $26 million is derived from the EPA Great Lakes Restoration Initiative.

[79] See http://www.asiancarp.us/news/2012frameworkreleased.htm; of the total, $19.4 million was to come from the EPA Great Lakes Restoration Initiative.

[80] The detailed 2011 framework is available online. See Asian Carp Regional Coordinating Committee, *2011 Asian Carp Control Strategy Framework*, December 2010, http://www.asiancarp.org/Documents/FrameworkDec15-2010.pdf.

Actions in the framework are generally uncontroversial and support or increase funding for most pre-2010 efforts, including the ongoing operation of the electric barriers, monitoring (both conventional and eDNA), and rapid response actions. The framework also supports a number of new actions and studies that may impede the spread of Asian carp, such as studies by the USGS to attract or repel the spread of Asian carp through pheromones or disruption of spawning, and funding to increase the commercial viability of Asian carp.

Hydrologic Separation

Separation of the Great Lakes and Mississippi River basins so as to prevent the interbasin movement of aquatic nuisance species is one prevention option that has recently received attention.[81] Permanent hydrologic separation of the basins in the Chicago area would make further encroachment of Asian carp in the area unlikely, but would also involve significant changes to existing navigation structures and operations in the CAWS.

Recently the Corps of Engineers began to evaluate options to prevent or reduce the spread of aquatic invasive species between the Great Lakes and Mississippi River basins. Congress authorized this study, now known as the Great Lakes Mississippi River Interbasin Study (GLMRIS), in WRDA 2007.[82] According to the Obama Administration, the technologies to be considered under the GLMRIS will include but are not limited to physical separation, as well as temporary or permanent lock closure.[83] The study is expected to be conducted in two phases: Focus Area I, expected to be completed in 2015, will evaluate options in the CAWS. Focus Area II, with an unknown completion date, will concentrate on other pathways. In its FY2012 budget justifications, the Corps estimated the total cost for both studies to be $25.5 million.[84]

Litigation

The apparent ecological and economic threat posed by the migration of Asian carp into the Great Lakes via the CAWS has prompted litigation to prevent such risks. Several Great Lakes states, particularly Michigan, have pursued a number of legal options, seeking court orders to restrict the entry of Asian carp into Lake Michigan and the Great Lakes generally.

In December 2009, Michigan petitioned the U.S. Supreme Court to amend its 1967 decree regarding diversion of water between Lake Michigan and the Illinois Waterway, including the Chicago Sanitary and Ship Canal.[85] With the support of other Great Lakes state and regional

---

[81] See also Jerry L. Rasmussen, et al., "Dividing the Waters: The Case for Hydrologic Separation of the North American Great Lakes and Mississippi River Basins," *Journal of Great Lakes Research*, v. 37, no. 3 (Sept 2011): 588-592.

[82] P.L. 110-114, § 345.

[83] 2011 Framework, p. 22.

[84] Assuming enactment of its FY2012 request for this study, the Corps projects $17.8 million remains to complete the study after FY2012. See FY2012 Budget Justifications, U.S. Army Corps of Engineers, p. LRD-70. Available at http://www.usace.army.mil/CECW/PID/Documents/j_sheets/just_2012.pdf.

[85] Motion to Reopen and For a Supplemental Decree, Petition, and Brief and Appendix in Support of Motion, *Wisconsin v. Illinois*, 388 U.S. 426 (1967), *available at* http://www.supremecourt.gov/SpecMastRpt/ Orig%201,%202%20&%203%20Motion%20to%20Reopen.pdf. The Court's 1967 decree controls the diversion of water from Lake Michigan into the Chicago Sanitary and Ship Canal and provides that any of the parties to the disputes resolved by the decree may petition the Court to modify the decree or issue a supplemental decree for issues that would (continued...)

---

governments, Michigan sought an order from the Court that would declare the operation of diversion facilities within the CAWS to be a public nuisance that threatened natural resources and allowed the introduction of invasive species into Lake Michigan.[86] Michigan also requested that the Court order Illinois, the U.S. Army Corps of Engineers, and the Metropolitan Water Reclamation District of Greater Chicago to prevent the spread of Asian carp into the lake by closing shipping locks and taking other necessary measures to prevent the carp from entering Lake Michigan.[87] Without comment, the Court denied Michigan's requests.[88] In February 2010, Michigan renewed its motion and requested that the Court reconsider an order to close the Chicago-area locks based on new evidence showing Asian carp to be present in Lake Michigan.[89] The Court again denied Michigan's motion without comment.[90]

After a live Asian carp was found beyond the electric barrier in the summer of 2010, Michigan, Minnesota, Ohio, Pennsylvania, and Wisconsin sued the U.S. Army Corps of Engineers and the Metropolitan Water Reclamation District of Greater Chicago (MWRD) in federal district court, seeking similar remedial measures as they requested in their attempt to amend the Supreme Court's 1967 decree. The states sought an order compelling the Corps and MWRD to abate the public nuisance created by the migration of Asian carp into the Great Lakes, to minimize the risk of migration from the CAWS to Lake Michigan, and to implement permanent measures to separate Illinois waters from Lake Michigan.[91] The court rejected each of the proposed remedial measures, noting a lack of consensus on the extent of the threat and the efficacy of the proposed solutions.[92] It held that the discovery of a live fish above the barrier did not prove that the barrier had failed and noted that the cause of the introduction of the fish to that particular section of the waterway was not known.[93] The court emphasized "its recognition that the potential harm in a worst case scenario is great" but concluded that "the level of certainty of harm is low based on the evidence adduced to date."[94]

(...continued)

affect the operation of the waterway. *Wisconsin*, 388 U.S. at 430.

[86] *Mot. to Reopen* at 1-2. Minnesota, New York, Ohio, Wisconsin, and the Canadian Province of Ontario filed briefs in support of Michigan's request.

[87] Motion for Preliminary Injunction at 29-30, *Wisconsin v. Illinois*, 388 U.S. 426.

[88] Wisconsin v. Illinois, Nos. 1, 2, and 3, Orig., 130 S.Ct. 1166 (Jan. 19, 2010) (order denying Michigan's motion for preliminary injunction); Wisconsin v. Illinois, Nos. 1, 2, and 3, Orig., 130 S.Ct. 2397 (Apr. 26, 2010) (order denying Michigan's motion to reopen and for supplemental decree).

[89] Renewed Motion for Preliminary Injunction, *Wisconsin v. Illinois*, 388 U.S. 426, *available at* http://www.supremecourt.gov/SpecMastRpt/1-Renewed%20Motion%20for%20PI.pdf.

[90] Wisconsin v. Illinois, Nos. 1, 2, and 3, Orig., 130 S.Ct. 1934 (Mar. 22, 2010) (order denying Michigan's renewed motion for preliminary injunction).

[91] Complaint for Injunctive and Declaratory Relief at 2, Michigan v. U.S. Army Corps of Engineers, No. 1:10-cv-04457 (N.D. Ill. July 19, 2010).

[92] Michigan v. U.S. Army Corps of Engineers, No. 1:10-cv-04457, 11-21 (filed Dec. 2, 2010), *available at* http://www.greatlakeslaw.org/files/dist_ct_pi_opinion_order.pdf.

[93] *Id.* at 49-50 ("the presence of a single live fish (or a small number of individual live fish) above the barrier is far too thin a basis from which to infer that the barrier is not effective").

[94] *Id.* at 54, 61.

Canadian Concern

For many decades, the United States and Canada have conducted a major cooperative program to deal with the consequences arising from the introduction of the non-native sea lamprey, *Petromyzon marinus*, to the Great Lakes. Through the Great Lakes Fishery Commission, the governments of the United States and Canada, together with neighboring states and provinces, spend millions of dollars annually to control this invasive parasite and limit its damage to sport and commercial fisheries.

Canada has assessed the risks posed by the introduction of Asian carp,[95] concluding that the risk of impact would be high in some parts of Canada, including the southern Great Lakes basin, by the four species of Asian carp. Canada is currently addressing these concerns through its participation in the bilateral Great Lakes Fishery Commission.

Congressional Interest

As previously mentioned, Section 126, Title I, of P.L. 111-85 directed the Corps to implement additional measures to prevent aquatic nuisance species from bypassing the Chicago Sanitary and Ship Canal Dispersal Barrier Project and to prevent aquatic nuisance species from dispersing into the Great Lakes. The 111th Congress held several hearings on Asian carp. On February 9, 2010, the House Transportation and Infrastructure Subcommittee on Water Resources and Environment held a hearing on Asian carp in the Great Lakes. On February 25, 2010, the Senate Energy and Natural Resources Subcommittee on Water and Power held a hearing to examine the science and policy behind efforts to prevent the introduction of Asian carp into the Great Lakes. On July 14, 2010, the Senate Energy and Natural Resources Subcommittee on Water and Power held an oversight hearing to examine the federal response to the discovery of Asian carp in Lake Calumet, Illinois.

Current Legislation

In the 112th Congress, Section 105, Division B, of P.L. 112-74 authorized the Corps of Engineers to take emergency measures to exclude Asian carp from the Great Lakes. In addition, H.R. 892 and S. 471 would direct the Corps of Engineers, U.S. Geological Survey, and FWS to take measures to control the spread of Asian carp. Notably, each of these bills, as well as H.R. 4406 and S. 2317, would require the Corps of Engineers to complete the Chicago portion of the aforementioned study on hydrologic separation (the Great Lakes and Mississippi River Interbasin Study, or GLMRIS) within 18 months of enactment. The Corps previously estimated 2015 as the completion date for this phase of the study. H.R. 2432 would require the Corps of Engineers to prepare an economic impact statement before carrying out any federal action relating to the Chicago Area Water System. H.R. 4146 and S. 2164 would authorize the Army Corps of Engineers to take actions to manage Asian carp traveling up the Mississippi River in the state of Minnesota.

---

[95] Available at http://www.dfo-mpo.gc.ca/csas/Csas/DocREC/2004/RES2004_103_E.pdf.

Funding and Authority for Ongoing Actions

A potential issue for the 112th Congress is funding for ongoing response actions related to Asian carp. As previously noted, funding for Asian carp response actions increased significantly in 2010 and 2011. Most of this funding (more than $84 million of an estimated $122 million) was announced in the Asian Carp Control Framework and has been provided through interagency transfers from the EPA's Great Lakes Restoration Initiative. In the most recent version of the Asian Carp Control Framework, the Regional Coordinating Committee noted that in FY2012 and beyond, ongoing Asian carp response activities will shift out of the GLRI and into agencies' base budgets.[96] However, it is not known how this change will impact these ongoing response actions, especially in light of constrained agency budgets and an uncertain fiscal climate.

An additional issue for Congress is the potential need for new authorities for agencies to undertake preventative measures. As previously mentioned, under Section 126 of the enacted appropriations bill for FY2010 (P.L. 111-85), Congress provided the Corps with one-year authority to implement emergency actions as necessary to prevent invasive species encroachment through the CAWS. This authority expired at the end of FY2010. The Corps has noted that to implement new actions, it may require an extension of the Section 126 authority for one or more years.[97] Additionally, the Corps may request an expansion in scope of the previous authority to allow for new prevention efforts outside the CAWS.

Author Contact Information

Eugene H. Buck
Specialist in Natural Resources Policy
gbuck@crs.loc.gov, 7-7262

Harold F. Upton
Analyst in Natural Resources Policy
hupton@crs.loc.gov, 7-2264

Charles V. Stern
Specialist in Natural Resources Policy
cstern@crs.loc.gov, 7-7786

Cynthia Brougher
Legislative Attorney
cbrougher@crs.loc.gov, 7-9121

---

[96] 2011 Framework, p. ES-1.

[97] In-person meeting with Ernest Drott, Corps of Engineers. December 17, 2010.

www.ingramcontent.com/pod-product-compliance
Lightning Source LLC
Chambersburg PA
CBHW082205290526
45794CB00008B/3424

9 781480 151833